JOSEPH HAYDN

THE CREATION

In a New Translation
by
ROBERT SHAW & ALICE PARKER

A division of
WARNER BROS. PUBLICATIONS

THE *Creation* of Haydn was written in 1797-1798, at the culminating point of his great decade of composition. These years had been spent largely in England: he had composed the magnificent *London Symphonies,* and had listened, deeply moved, to performances of Handel's choral works. On his return to Vienna, he asked his friend Baron van Swieten to translate into German an English libretto which had been given him by one Linley, who had prepared it from Milton's *Paradise Lost* and from *Genesis.* Haydn composed the music to this German text, and the first performance in 1798, with Haydn himself conducting, was sung in German. This same Baron van Swieten then retranslated the text into English with rather considerable changes in the duration and accentuation of Haydn's phrases, and, according to Tovey, "not without refreshing details in the style of 'English as She is Spoke'." The present translation is an attempt not only to repair the *"disjecta membra* of the Linley-van-Swieten-English-as-She-is-Spoke confection," but to unite Haydn's minutely picturesque musical language with the colorful and understandable English text which it deserves.

Sir Donald Francis Tovey, in his essay on the *Creation,* gives a clear picture of the scope and purpose of the work. "The words of the Bible are divided between three archangels, Raphael, Uriel, and Gabriel, and a chorus which, throughout the whole work, may be considered as that of the heavenly hosts. The list and description of created things is not distributed haphazardly among the three archangels: Uriel is distinctly the angel of the sun and of daylight; his is the tenor voice, and his is the description of Man. Raphael sings of the earth and the sea, of the beginning of all things . . . the description of the beasts, the great whales, and 'every living creature that moveth'; and it is he who reports God's blessing, 'Be fruitful and multiply.' in a measured passage which is one of the sublimest incidents in Haydn's recitatives. Gabriel, the soprano, leads the heavenly hosts and describes the vegetable kingdom and the world of bird life.

Lastly, Adam and Eve appear and fulfill the purpose announced by Raphael while as yet 'the work was not complete; theere wanted yet that wondrous being, who God's design might thankful see, and grant His goodness joyful praise.' Or, as the first answer in the Shorter Catechism has it,

> Q. What is the chief end of Man?
> A. To glorify God and to enjoy Him for ever."

— *Robert Shaw and Alice Parker*

SOLO VOICES:

Sopranos: Gabriel, Eve   *Tenor:* Uriel

Basses: Raphael, Adam

INDEX

PART THE FIRST

PART THE SECOND

PART THE THIRD

THE CREATION

PART THE FIRST

Joseph Haydn

1. INTRODUCTION (REPRESENTATION OF CHAOS)

6

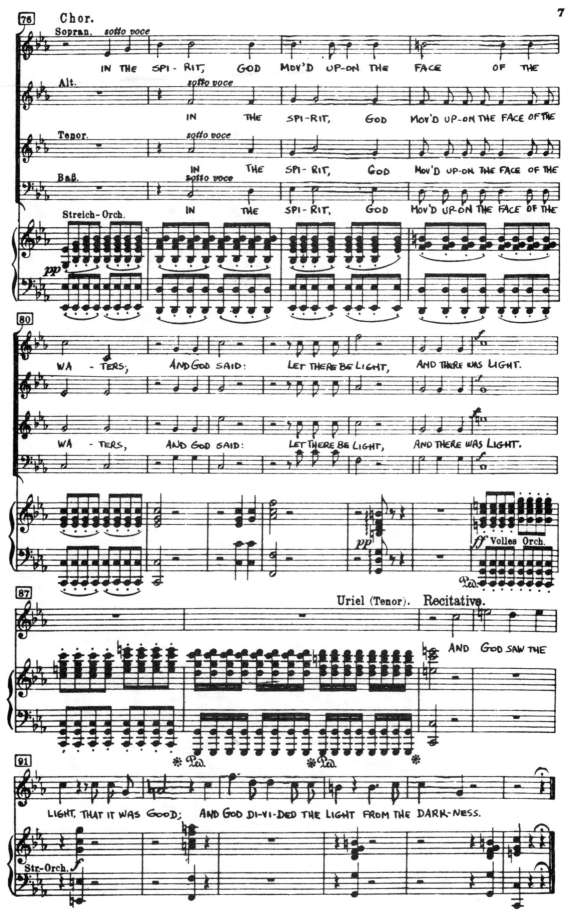

8

2. ARIA WITH CHORUS

NOW VAN-ISH'D BY THE HO - LY BEAMS

THE AN-CIENT, GHOST-LY, SHUD-DER-ING BLACKNESS

NOW VAN-ISH'D BY THE

HO - LY BEAMS THE AN-CIENT GHOST-LY SHUD-DER-ING

L.G.Co.51595

10

L.G.Co.51595

3. RECITATIVE

Raphael.

AND GOD MADE THE FIR-MA-MENT, AND DI-VI-DED THE WA-TERS WHICH WERE UN-DER THE

Cembalo.

FIR-MA-MENT FROM THE WA-TERS WHICH WERE A-BOVE THE FIR-MA-MENT: AND IT WAS SO.

Allegro assai.

f Orchester.

THEN HOWL-ING RAGED THE BLAST OF THE TEM-PEST,

4. SOLO AND CHORUS

24

5. RECITATIVE

6. ARIA

80

7. RECITATIVE

L.G.Co.51595

8. ARIA

9. RECITATIVE

10. CHORUS

36

40

L.G.Co.51595

11. RECITATIVE

Uriel.

AND GOD SAID, LET THERE BE LIGHTS IN THE FIR-MA-MENT OF HEAV'N, TO DI-

VIDE THE DAY FROM THE NIGHT, TO GIVE THEIR LIGHT UP-ON THE

EARTH; AND LET THEM BE FOR SIGNS AND FOR SEA-SONS, AND FOR DAYS AND FOR

YEARS. HE MADE THE STARS AL-SO.

SPLEN - - - DOR AND LIGHT, WITH SPLEN-DOR AND LIGHT.

L.G.Co.51595

42

12. RECITATIVE

13. CHORUS WITH SOLI

46

48

51

52

54

End of the First Part

14. RECITATIVE

15. ARIA

58

60

61

L.G.Co.51595

16. RECITATIVE

AND GOD CRE-A-TED GREAT WHALES, AND EV-'RY LIV - ING CREA-TURE THAT

MOV-ETH; AND GOD BLESSED THEM, SAY-ING: BE FRUIT-FUL

17. RECITATIVE

Raphael.

AND THE AN-GELS STRUCK THEIR IM-MOR-TAL HARPS AND SANG THE WON-DERS, AND SANG THE WON-DERS OF THE FIFTH DAY.

18. TRIO

Moderato. *cantabile*

attacca

19. TRIO AND CHORUS

76

L.G.Co.51595

20. RECITATIVE

21. RECITATIVE

BOUND-ING WITH BRANCH-ING HEAD, THE NIM-BLE STAG.

WITH SNORT-ING AND

staccato

STAMP-ING, FLY-ING MANE, UP-REARS IN MIGHT THE NO-BLE STEED.

Andante.

Fl.

IN

p

staccato

PLEA-SANT PAS-TURES, QUI-ET-LY THE CAT-TLE GRAZE ON MEA-DOWS GREEN.

p

Fl. u. Fag.

AND

23. RECITATIVE

24. ARIA

88

27. TRIO

96

L.G.Co.51595

98

L.G.Co.51595

28. CHORUS

106

End of the Second Part

PART THE THIRD

29. RECITATIVE

110

L.G.Co.51595

112

120

L.G.Co.51595

122

124

126

L.G.Co.51595

130

31. DUET RECITATIVE

32. DUET

134

SOFT - LY FLY THE GOLD-EN HOURS,— EV'- RY MO - MENT IS

RAP-TURE, IS RAP-TURE, NAUGHT OF SAD-NESS, NAUGHT OF SAD-NESS LIN - GERS

NEAR. SWEET COM-PAN-ION! EV'- RY MO - MENT IS RAP-TURE, NAUGHT OF

SAD-NESS LIN - -GERS NEAR. DEAR - - -EST HUS-BAND! HERE BE-

SIDE THEE, FLOODS OF JOY O'ER-FLOW MY HEART: THAT THOU—

L.G.Co.51595

136

138

140

L.G.Co.51595

142

L.G.Co.51595

144

33. RECITATIVE

34. FINAL CHORUS WITH SOLI

L.G.Co.51595

146

L.G.Co.51595

147

L.G.Co.51595

152

L.G.Co.51595

End